MEMOIR

OF

NATHANIEL MACON

OF

NORTH CAROLINA

BY

WELDON N. EDWARDS

Foreword by Dr. Boyd D. Cathey

Memoir of Nathaniel Macon of North Carolina

By Weldon N. Edwards

Originally published by the Raleigh Register Steam Power Press, Raleigh, North Carolina, in 1862

Foreword by Dr. Boyd D. Cathey

©2014 The Scuppernong Press

First Printing

The Scuppernong Press
PO Box 1724
Wake Forest, NC 27588
www.scuppernongpress.com

Cover and book design by Frank B. Powell, III

All rights reserved. Printed in the United States of America.

No part of this book may be reproduced or transmitted in any form or by any means, electronic or mechanical, including photocopying, recording, or by any information and storage and retrieval system, without written permission from the editor and/or publisher.

International Standard Book Number ISBN 978-0-9898399-3-8

Library of Congress Control Number: 2014936872

Contents

Introduction --- *iii*

Foreword --- *v*

Illustration of Nathaniel Macon -------------------------- *xii*

Author's Preface --- *xv*

Memoir of Nathaniel Macon of North Carolina ------- 1

Note -- 19

Illustrations --- 23

~ Introduction ~

Almost forgotten by today's so-called historians, Nathaniel Macon still stands as one of the most important figures in the early years of the United States. A contemporary of Thomas Jefferson and John Randolph of Roanoke, he was highly thought of by friends and adversaries alike. President Jefferson called him *Ultimus Romanorum*, the last of the Romans.

Macon was a staunch conservative, an agrarian and a proponent of states' rights. A veteran of the Revolutionary War, he is the only North Carolinian to serve as speaker of the House of Representatives. He was also very unassuming, not even wanting a marker on his grave site, just a pile of rocks he had collected on his farm. However, many towns, cities and counties across the country, especially in the South, are named for him.

Perhaps this is why he is virtuality unknown today. This memoir was written almost 30 years after his passing by a friend during a time of war and Macon probably would have wished it was not published. But, it was published and it is a good example of a Confederate imprint. The fact this was published during the middle of the War for Southern Independence shows the importance of the subject matter. Supplies were hard to come by and the author even apologizes for the quality of the paper it was printed on.

This reprint has been reset in a modern typeface with all the original grammar and syntax intact. This introduction, the foreword and images are added in this edition. Thanks to Dr. Cathey for his encouragement and insightful thoughts in the foreword.

We hope you enjoy our efforts and please pass along the memory of Nathaniel Macon of North Carolina.

— Frank B. Powell, III, Editor

Foreword

Back in 1975 the Warren County [N.C.] Historical Association initiated a comprehensive project to study the life and legacy of Nathaniel Macon. As a part of this project, both archaeological and architectural studies of his old Buck Spring plantation, near the Roanoke River, were commissioned. Working with the professional staff of the North Carolina Division of Archives and History, the Macon project had, it was proposed at the time, a longer range potential objective: a possible state historic site to honor North Carolina's most historically significant political leader, whose legacy and philosophy and character influenced not only generations of Tar Heels, but also a host of very illustrious Southerners, their thinking, and the very manner in which they lived their lives and viewed the society around them.

Working with architectural historians and experienced archaeologists, I was commissioned to prepare both a chain of title for the Buck Spring site, as well as a detailed written history of Macon and his life. All of this would be organized in a major report which might be used to justify the future creation of an important historic site, sadly never realized, giving credit finally to this giant of North Carolina and American history. At that time I was finishing up a doctorate in graduate school. A few years earlier Macon and his under appreciated significance to the history of this nation had figured in my MA thesis presented at the University of Virginia. I was amazed at the incredible importance "the Squire of Buck Spring" had had in the new American nation, and, more interestingly, the influence he had on such later and much better known figures as John C. Calhoun and President John Tyler.

Yet, in 1975 Macon was basically unknown, and his role and importance in American history, so appreciated before the War Between the States, was largely ignored or glossed over.

Quite a bit of this contemporary ignorance must, I think, be attributed to Macon's philosophy. He was, indeed, to quote his contemporaries, "the father of states' rights" and the figure most critical in the actual development and survival of the states' rights philosophy that still, in some ways, percolates in American politics.

Above all, it was Macon's probity of character and his steadfast devotion to principle which won him general admiration from across the entire spectrum of antebellum political opinion. Leaders as diverse as Presidents John Quincy Adams and John Tyler expressed great admiration for Macon; many attempted to tie in their own views, even those ideas that seemed at odds with Macon's, to those of the Squire of Buck Spring. After leaving the US House of Representatives in 1816 and being elevated to the United State Senate by the North Carolina General Assembly, Macon's influence only grew and became more pervasive, especially in the South.

It was his role during the debates over the Missouri Compromise which signaled the emergence of a genuine states' rights philosophy. But it was not just that hotly debated issue which occupied his attention. Questions regarding internal improvements, the establishment of a national bank, and the general role of the Federal government in questions hitherto considered the concern of states, also occupied him. For him all such issues, and increasingly the contentious issue of slavery, were a part of a larger question, that of how the Constitution was to be interpreted.

As early as March 1818 he wrote to North Carolina congressman Bartlett Yancey as follows:

I must ask you to examine the Constitution of the United States ... and tell me, if Congress can establish banks, make roads and canals, whether they cannot free all the slaves in the United States?... We have abolition, colonization and peace societies — their intentions cannot be known; but the character and spirit of one may without injustice be considered that of all. It is a charac-

ter and spirit of perseverance bordering on enthusiasm, and if the general government shall continue to stretch its powers, these societies will undoubtedly push it to try the question of emancipation....

With the debate over Missouri looming, Macon wrote to Bartlett again, in April 1818:

If Congress can make canals they can with more propriety emancipate. Be not deceived, I speak soberly in the fear of God and the love of the Constitution. Let not the love of improvement or a thirst for glory blind that sober discretion and sound sense, with which the Lord has blest you. Paul was not more anxious or sincere concerning Timothy, than I am for you. Your error in this will injure if not destroy our beloved mother, North Carolina, and all the South country. Add not to the Constitution nor take therefrom. Be not led astray by grand notions or magnificent opinions. Remember that you belong to a meek State and just people, who want nothing but to enjoy the fruits of their labor honestly and to lay out their profits in their own way.

In early 1819 the actual debate in the Senate over the admission of Missouri to the union commenced, and, as Missouri was a territory where slavery existed, that contentious question became central to the debate. A resolution — a compromise — put forward by Senator Jesse Thomas of Illinois proposed admitting Maine as a "free" state and Missouri as a "slave" state but prohibiting slavery in the rest of the Louisiana Purchase north of latitude 36 degrees, 30 minutes.

Many Southern leaders, including the then Secretary of War John C. Calhoun, were prepared to go along initially with the compromise, but Macon, singularly, rose to oppose it. And it was in his famous Senate speech on the question which heralded the birth of a full-fledged "Southern philosophy." The speech deserves to be quoted at length:

All the states now have equal rights and are content. Deprive one of the least right which it now enjoys in common with the others and it will no longer be content.... All the new states have the same rights that the old have; why make Missouri an exception? Why depart in her case from the great American principle that the people can govern themselves? All the country west of the Mississippi was acquired by the same treaty, and on the same terms and the people in every part have the same rights.... The [Thomas] amendment will operate unjustly to the people who have gone there from other states. They carried with them property [slaves] guaranteed by their states, by the Constitution and treaty; they purchased lands and settled on them without molestation; but now, unfortunately for them, it is discovered that they ought not to have been permitted to carry a single slave.... Let the United States abandon this new scheme; let their magnanimity, and not their power, be felt by the people of Missouri. **The attempt to govern too much has produced every civil war that ever has been, and will, probably, every one that ever may be.** [Bold added]

And finishing with an amazingly prescient vision of the future, Macon continued:

Why depart from the good old way? Why leave the road of experience to take this new one, of which we have no experience? This way leads to universal emancipation, of which we have no experience.... A clause in the Declaration of Independence has been read, declaring "that all men are created equal." Follow that sentiment, and does it not lead to universal emancipation? If it will justify putting an end to slavery in Missouri, will it not justify it in the old states? Suppose the plan followed, and all the slaves turned loose, and the union to continue, is it certain that the present Constitution would last long?

The debate over the Missouri Compromise marked a significant turning point in American history and, eventually, in the diverging views of the leaders of both the South and the North. Although Macon had been engaged in a losing effort to block the compromise, his forthright and clear-sighted defense of strict constructionism and his beloved "South country" had singled him out as a prophet. Not many years after his remarkable intervention in the Missouri debates, a whole generation of Southern congressmen and political leaders would acknowledge him as the intellectual father of states' rights. In 1821 a chastened Thomas Jefferson, who had also foreseen how the crisis would affect the nation — Jefferson, who termed the stark reality made visible by the debates as "a fire bell in the night" — called Macon "the Depositor of old & sound principles," and wrote him: "God bless you & long continue your wholesome influence in public councils."

Despite his staunch support for states' rights and "old republicanism," Macon was greatly esteemed by a wide variety of American political leaders. President John Quincy Adams, a man of almost diametrically opposite views, in his *Memoirs* described Macon as "…a stern republican … a man of stern parts and mean education, but of rigid integrity, and a blunt, though not offensive, deportment … one of the most influential members of the Senate. His integrity, his indefatigable attention to business, and his long experience give him a weight of character and consideration which few men of superior minds ever acquire." In 1828 it was widely rumored that Adams, despite differences with Macon, considered him as his potential vice-presidential choice.

In 1824, after the illness of leading states' rights presidential candidate, William H. Crawford, Governor George M. Troup of Georgia put forward Macon as a candidate for president: "I know of no person who would unite so extensively the public sentiment of the southern country … as yourself." In 1825 Macon received twenty-four electoral votes for the vice-presidency. In 1826 and 1827 he was elected President Pro-Tempore of the United States Senate.

As he approached the end of his long career, recognition of his significant role in American history and political development came from some of the most significant voices of the time. From Calhoun, John Tyler and Thomas Hart Benton came encomiums and words of admiration and the recognition that Macon had played a pivotal role in the history of the first sixty years of the American nation.

While many readers in our modern age may think Macon's most pointed comments deal with the institution of slavery, it was not defending the "peculiar institution" which was at the base of his philosophy. Indeed, his stringent commentary on the Federal bank and government support for internal improvements equally reflect a states' rights consistency and integrity. Slavery, because Macon recognized it as a particularly dangerous lynchpin for the American nation, certainly occupied a salient part of his commentary. But the greater issue for him was the growing power and control of the Federal government and the eventual destruction of the older Constitutional system erected by the Founders.

In 1835, in his last major public role, Macon was elected to preside over the North Carolina Constitutional Convention. While he made few interventions, he generally opposed changes to the state constitution. For him, "all changes in government were from better to worse."

In June 1837 Macon summoned his doctor and the undertaker and paid them in advance. He died on June 29 that year, at Buck Spring. In a simple ceremony on his plantation he was interred, attended by grieving slaves, with whom he had worked side-by-side in his fields. He instructed his executor and son-in-law, the Honorable Weldon N. Edwards, that no monument mark his grave, but that a pile of smooth stones be placed upon the site.

His epitaph he spoke eighteen years earlier, in Congress: "The attempt to govern too much has produced every civil war that ever has been, and will, probably, every one that ever may be." Macon understood and clearly foresaw the results of the destruction of liberties and the erosion of states' rights and the emergence of an all-encompassing Federal government.

The pile of stones at Buck Spring remains, as does the philosophy that Macon first enunciated, despite the accomplishment of the shattering prophecy he uttered. And, now, it is up to another generation to attempt to retrieve and recover the Founders' vision.

— Dr. Boyd D. Cathey

Nathaniel Macon
Collection of the US House of Representatives

MEMOIR

OF

NATHANIEL MACON

OF

NORTH CAROLINA

BY
WELDON N. EDWARDS

RALEIGH
RALEIGH REGISTER STEAM POWER PRESS
1862

To Wm. Eaton, Jr.:

SIR — Knowing the profound veneration and abiding affection always entertained by you for your grandfather, the late N. Macon, of North Carolina; and persuaded that his virtues and principles have found a worthy representative in the grandson, I feel a pride in addressing to you the following pages. Their preparation has been, to me, "a labor of love," and I indulge the hope that I have presented his character fairly and truthfully to the world, and placed before the American youth the model of a statesman and patriot that will challenge admiration throughout all time. I take great pleasure in the opportunity the occasion affords of assuring you of the high consideration and cordial esteem and regard,

    With which I am,

        Your friend,

            W. N. EDWARDS.

Poplar Mount, N.C. }
6th July, 1862.

It is proper that the Publisher of the following Memoir should state that the paper on which it is printed is not of as good quality as the Author desired. After a diligent search, however, it has been found to be the best in color and texture that can now be procured.

The Copyright of the Memoir, as will be seen, has been secured; but not for the pecuniary benefit of its Author, whose sole object in writing it was, to pay a tribute of admiration and respect to the memory of one of the purest and best men that ever lived in any age or country.

PUBLISHER.

MEMOIR OF NATHANIEL MACON.

It is cause of profound thankfulness, that the good and the wise, with whose presence we are blessed in this life, to guide us in the paths of virtue, when they are no more, leave behind them lessons and examples full of instruction. To give to these enduring form, and to hold them up as a mirror of life, by a truthful picture of the lives and manners of their authors, is a service of inappreciable value to mankind; and, at the same time, but a just tribute to the illustrious dead. The subject of this memoir may be justly classed among those whose virtues deserve to be thus commemorated.

NATHANIEL MACON was born on the 17th of December, 1758, in the county of Bute, of the then province of North Carolina, in that part of it now Warren, within a few miles of the present village of Warrenton, of poor and respectable parents. His great-grandfather was a Huegonot, and came over from France to escape the persecutions consequent upon the revocation of the Edict of Nantz, in 1685. His father, Gideon H. Macon, was born in Virginia, whence he came to North Carolina. His mother was a native of North Carolina, and a daughter of Edward Jones, of Shocco. He lost his father in early boyhood, and was left, with many brothers and sisters, in the care of his widowed mother, with such moderate means of support as to require the utmost care and industry to get on even tolerably in the world. He assisted in all the domestic offices and labors common with boys at that day. He acquired the rudiments of education in the neighborhood, at what was then called an "Old-field School." The application, progress and good habits of the boy gave such promise of the future man, that it was resolved to make every effort to give him a thorough education; and he was accordingly sent to Princeton College, New Jersey. His own inclinations eagerly seconded the hopeful purpose of his friends. While there, he prosecuted his studies with fond diligence, and sought all the avenues to useful knowledge with unflagging zeal. Nor did he relax his efforts in this respect after his return home — devoting to such books as were within his reach all the time he could spare from the ordinary duties of life; but he met with great difficulties, owing to the scarcity of books and his own poverty. In the latter part of his life, he was often heard to say, that his eyesight failed him sooner than it otherwise would have done, in consequence of his reading so much by fire-light in his youth and early manhood — being then too poor to buy candles — his small patrimony having been exhausted during his minority in his support and education.

His love for North Carolina was sincere and thorough. In all that concerned her character — her institutions — her welfare, he felt an ever wakeful solicitude. Although he received his collegiate education in a distant State, he ever after gave a decided preference to the seminaries of his own loved North Carolina. When his son-in-law, William Eaton, Sen'r, in the year 1828, was about to send two of his sons to Cambridge, he dissuaded him from it, and advised him to send them to the University of North Carolina; because, among other reasons, they would there make acquaintances of many of the future men of the State, and contract friendships that would be of service to them in the part they were destined to act in the great drama of life.

He studied law, but never applied for a license to practice. There is now in the possession of his grandson, William Eaton, Jr., (who shared all his confidence and affections, and is a worthy representative of his principles and virtues,) an old London-bound edition of *Blackstone's Commentaries*, which was used by him, and which is highly valued as a family relict. Like all persons of taste, he admired the classic elegance of this celebrated work, but regarded its author as too subservient to power, and wanting in manliness and independence. He considered Sir Edward Coke a much better friend to English liberty.

He exhibited in early life those qualities which subsequently established for him a spotless and enduring fame, and which rendered his character one of the brightest ornaments of North Carolina and the Union.

> *"Incorrupta fides nuclaque Veritas,*
> *Mens conscia Recti,"*

were then, as ever afterwards, his distinguishing characteristics.

Mr. Macon was one of the few patriots of the American Revolution, who survived to his time to tell the trials of that eventful period. In the memorable year 1776, then not 18 years old, and while a student at Princeton, New Jersey — burning with youthful ardor, and fired by holy enthusiasm in the cause of public liberty — he abandoned his collegiate duties, and performed a short tour of military duty in a company of volunteers, on the Delaware — thus evincing in his youth, an attachment to those principles, which, in after life, he supported with so much firmness, ability and undeviating consistency. This service over, he returned to college. In 1779, seeing the war-cloud gathering in his own dear South, and its conquest seriously threatened, he hastened home and joined the militia troops of his native State as a common soldier; and continued with them till the provisional articles of peace were signed in November, 1782. While in this trying, though to him grateful service, he gave proofs of that indifference for office and emolument, and that unaffected devotedness to his country's good, which his future history so conspicuously illustrated. He served in the ranks during the whole period, as a common soldier; and though command and places of trust and confidence, as well as of ease and safety, were often tendered him, he invariably declined them — desiring only to occupy the station and share the hardships and perils common to the greatest portion of his fellows-soldiers; and although in very humble circumstances, as to property, he never would charge or consent to receive, nor did he ever receive, one cent for such services. He gave his heart and soul to the cause in which he had embarked; he loved his country, and, like a dutiful son, gave her in time of need — '"twas all he had" — his personal services. And when that country — blessed with the smiles of prosperity, had grown to power and wealth, and, with a munificence deserving all praise, made liberal provision for the soldiers of the Revolution, still did he decline the proffered bounty. Often has he been heard to say, disclaiming all imputation upon others, that no state of fortune could induce him to accept it. In those times, too, were developed the noble traits of Roman character which attracted to him the confidence and esteem of his countrymen. He became generally known throughout the State, and won for himself a popularity, to which his country is indebted for his long and useful and illustrious services in the public councils.

His countrymen elected him, while yet in the army, and scarcely twenty-three years old, a member of the State Legislature, without his solicitation or even knowledge; and reluctant to part with his comrades in arms, his first impulse was to decline this new service. This coming to the ears of General Green, in whose camp he was at the time stationed, on the left bank of the Yadkin, when the sudden flooding of that river arrested the pursuit of Cornwallis; he sent for the young soldier — earnestly remonstrated with him — and finally succeeded in persuading him that he could do more good as a member of the General Assembly than as a soldier. He saw it at once. 'Twas his country that called, and he readily obeyed the summons of the Governor to his new theatre of duty. After serving in this capacity many years, he was chosen, at the age of thirty-two, a member of Congress, in the House of Representatives, and took his seat at the 1st Session of the 2nd Congress, in 1791, which he filled uninterruptedly, under successive elections, till the winter of 1815-'16, when he was chosen by the legislature a Senator in Congress — without his solicitation, and, in one sense, against his wish; for his maxim was, "frequent elections and accountability at short intervals," and that accountability to *the people*.

With a firm reliance upon the constancy of the people, and their pure and unsophisticated judgment, guided by the promptings of interest to do right, he was fully persuaded that rectitude of conduct had nothing to fear from such an ordeal.

In January, 1816, being then at Washington in the discharge of his duties as member of the House of Representatives, he resigned his seat in that body and assumed his new station as Senator. On that occasion he declined and rejected double pay for traveling, although abundant precedents entitled him to it. The legislature continued to him this honorable distinction and high trust till, induced by a sense of duty "from impaired health and waning memory," he resigned in November, 1828 — resigning at the same time the offices of Justice of the Peace and Trustee of the University of North Carolina, both of which he had filled for many years.

During his congressional career he was elected Speaker of the House of Representatives at the 1st Session of the 7th Congress, in 1801; and continued to preside over the deliberations of that body until the 10th Congress, when, not being able to attend at its commencement, from severe indisposition, a new incumbent was chosen. The duties of the chair were discharged by him with distinguished ability and impartiality, which secured the esteem and affection of his political friends, and won the confidence and admiration of his political adversaries. He was often elected President of the Senate, and the last time chosen to that station, courteously and unostentatiously declined its acceptance. The office of Postmaster General was twice tendered him, and in 1824 the use of his name as a candidate for the Vice-Presidency was strongly solicited; but office, however high, or emolument however great, had no charms for him. His engagement was always to his *constituents*, and *that* he was determined to fulfill to the letter. No lure could tempt him to lay it down. His was the ambition that prompted only to virtuous deeds. He sought, with great earnestness and untiring industry, the path of duty, and fearlessly pursued it — obliging no one from favor or affection, and yielding nothing to the suggestions of resentment or passion. Indeed, there was no passion he would gratify at the expense of duty. In 1835, his fellow-citizens again called him from his cherished retirement, by electing him a member of the Convention, charged with the important duty of revising and reforming the Constitution of his native State — of which body he was chosen President by unanimous suffrage. In 1836, he was chosen Elector of President and Vice-President, on the Republican ticket, and at the proper time repaired to the seat of government and performed the duty required of him — presiding at the same time over the deliberations of the College. This was the closing act of Mr. Macon's public life. Ho was spared to his country but a few months longer.

Of his political creed, it is scarcely necessary to speak. His *unchequered consistency* — *the frank and manly avowal of his opinions* on all proper occasions — *the prominent and distinguished part* it was his lot to act in support of every Republican administration — sufficiently proclaim it. Suffice it to say, he was a Republican of the Old School; and possessed, without qualification or abatement, the affection and confidence of a JEFFERSON, a MADISON, a MONROE, and a JACKSON, and of the whole host of distinguished statesmen, with whom he was a co-laborer in the cause of democracy and free government. His political principles were deep-rooted. He became attached to them from early examination, and was confirmed in their correctness from mature reason and long experience. They were the principles of genuine Republicanism; and to them, through life, he gave a hearty, consistent, and available support. With them he never compromised; and the greater the pressure, the more pertinaciously he stood by them. Adopting, to the fullest extent, the doctrine which allowed to man the capacity for, and the right of self-government — *he* was a strict constructionist of the Constitution of the United States, and never would consent — however strongly the law of circumstances, the common plea of tyrants, might demand it — to exercise doubtful powers. Jealous of Federal authority, his most vigilant efforts were directed towards restraining it within due limits. A democrat by nature as well as by education, he was persuaded, — that on the popular part of every government depend its real force — its welfare — its security — its permanence— its adaptation to the happiness of the people.

Stability and consistency were strong points in Mr. Macon's character — formed upon his uncompromising adherence to principle and unswerving fidelity to duty. In his conversation, easy and unaffected; in his manners and dress, a decided model of republican simplicity; pretentious in nothing; all who approached him felt conscious of receiving the civility and respect demanded by the nicest sense of propriety. To these characteristics did he owe much of that firm hold upon the confidence and esteem of his countrymen which sustained him in the severe trials always to be met in the great battle of life. His was an enduring popularity; it never waned; it existed in as much vigor and freshness at the close of his life as at any former period; it lived after him — and it is the source of the highest gratification to his numerous friends and admirers that he is still often quoted as the bright exemplar of *"the honest man and the wise and virtuous statesman.*" This feature in his life is the more striking when viewed in contrast with the political fortunes of others of the most exalted worth and eminent services, who failed to retain, to the last, that popular favor obviously due to their great merit and conspicuous usefulness. " 'Tis true, 'tis pity 'tis true," that popular favor is often lost without fault. The popular heart, whose aims are always right, is often swayed by the satan-like influences and ill-bred prejudices, manufactured by the selfish and designing, in workshops of iniquity — their own wicked brains — and the most patriotic and eminently useful, who deserve to be embalmed in the hearts of their countrymen, too often become victims to their vile practices.

Though so long honored, and so many years the depositary of public honors and public trusts, Mr. Macon's was the rare merit of never having solicited any one to vote for him, or even intimated a wish that he should; and though no one shared more fully the confidence of a large circle of influential friends, his is the praise of never having solicited the slightest interest for his own preferment. Public honors sought him; he prized them only as the reward of faithful and virtuous performance, and regarded place as the means merely of bringing him in nearer contact with public duty. He made no popular harangues, seeking to avoid the temptation of being betrayed into promises which he could not or would not fulfill, or into protestations which his heart would not sanction. He was never found rambling through his Congressional District, seeking to engineer himself into popular favor by means, which, self-respect and a just sense of the rights of others, forbade. His rule was to attend, punctually, once a year, if health permitted, the first court held in each county in his district after his return from Congress. There he met his constituents — there he received their greetings and heard their complaints — there, without simulation, gave a full account of his stewardship.

In his intercourse with them he was easy, frank and communicative — never withholding his opinions upon matters of pubic concernment, and always inviting them to the exercise of the utmost freedom of thought and of speech, as the highest privilege of freemen, and the surest guard of liberty. He never attended, what, in his own characteristic language, he called "a man-dinner," regarding all such as political pageants, with too much of deceptions exterior, and too little calculated to better the popular heart or enlighten the popular mind. And, when upon his retirement from Congress, a large portion of his old constituents tendered him the compliment of a public dinner, he declined it in a brief note, saying, that "he had never been at such a show, and that he had already received the most gratifying proofs of their good will and esteem."

To shun all ostentatious display and the emptiness of pride was, with him, a *principle*; and to do good to his fellow-men, and to society, a rule of action, which he scrupulously observed, always abstaining, in the employment of his faculties and in the use of the abundant goods with which frugal industry had blessed him, from the gratification of any passion, the indulgence of which prudence forbade to others less favored by fortune — thus teaching, by both precept and example, the necessity of temperance, frugality and industry, as the surest and best foundation for contentment and plenty.

Of generous and unsuspicious nature, he never looked with uncharitableness on the actions of his fellow men, but, with the strength and armor of a well balanced mind, gave to them the calmest consideration, and assigned to each its appropriate place in the scale of Good and Evil. Of philosophic mind, subdued temper, and great self-command, he met the incidents and accidents of life, not with stoic indifference, but with quiet submission — yielding nothing to passion, less to despondency, and looking to passing events as to a school for instruction, and deducing from them useful lessons to guide him in the pathway of life.

Of him it may be emphatically said, that he thought for himself, but reposing, with confidence, on his discriminating sense of justice and integrity of purpose, he gave to all subjects the fullest deliberation, and never jumped to conclusions in advance of his judgment. But when he had formed an opinion, he adhered to it with a fearless and virtuous inflexibility, which yielded to no importunity or persuasion. This, with some, subjected him to the charge of obstinacy.

"Virtus itself, 'scapes not calumnious strokes."

But, if this were a fault, it found a sanction in his unaffected love of justice, and evinced the absence of that facile disposition which too often betrays into error, by sacrificing to a spirit of accommodation for the sake of a seeming but culpable amiability. His maxim was, "No compromise of Right." He utterly rejected the doctrine "that the end sanctifies the means." He had his singularities, yet they were not such as to "blur the face of virtue," but, forming exceptions to the fashionable foibles and manners of the times, were rather bright spots in his character that gave to it greater beauty. He was no copyist. He o'ermastered custom's ways, and "dared to be what he thought he ought to be."

He was chary of promises, but always punctual and exact in performance; would give his bond or note to no man — contract no debts — would buy nothing without paying for it. "Pay as you go" was a law to him, which he inflexibly observed. He mastered all his wants, and kept them in strict subjection to reason. He would lend money to a friend, but never take interest. He classed labor among the Virtues — never called for help in anything he could do himself — labored often in his fields at the head of his slaves, during the intervals allowed from public duties, and topped all his own tobacco, when at home at the proper season, till the infirmities of age rendered him unable to stand the heat of the sun. He was fond of the chase, and indulged in his favorite amusement — the pursuit of the fox and the deer — as long as he lived.

He spoke often in Congress — seldom long. His speeches were always to the point; strong, practical, sententious — often furnishing materials for the rhetorical displays of others. A most distinguished member once characterized his speeches as "dishes of the best materials served up in the best manner." Unless prevented by bad health, he was always in his seat — voted on every question — was punctual in attendance upon committees, and ever ready at the call of duty.

He was fond of reading, but his favorite study was Man. "He made choice of human nature for the object of his thoughts." To this predilection, did he owe that consummate knowledge of the human character, and those practical lessons of wisdom of so much consequence in the conduct of life, which gave him rank among the "wisest and best."

There is no surer test of merit than is found in the favorable opinions of the wise and the good, formed in the unrestricted freedom of social intercourse, when the seal of reserve is unloosed, and neither the pride of ostentation nor the dread of criticism or censure, invites to concealment. Impressed with this truth, with a view to impart deeper interest to this sketch, by stamping the seal of verity upon the high and noble traits it portrays, recourse is had to the correspondence of eminent and distinguished statesmen to whom all the avenues of knowledge were opened by close intimacy, and long association in public life. *Thomas Jefferson*, whose monument is to be found in the Declaration of *Independence* and in the enduring popular veneration which he so largely shared, but a few weeks after his first inauguration as President of the United States in 1801 thus writes to Mr. Macon: "And in *all* cases, when an office becomes vacant in your State, as the distance would "occasion a great delay, were you to wait to be regularly consulted I shall be much obliged to you to recommend the best characters. There is nothing I am so anxious about as making the best possible appointments; and no case in which the best men are more liable to mislead us, by yielding to the solicitations of applicants. For this reason your own spontaneous recommendation would be desirable." Thus did Mr. J. stake an important portion of his administrative duties upon his high estimate of Mr. M.'s integrity and wisdom. Again, in another letter to Mr. Macon, the 24th March, 1826, Mr. Jefferson says: "My grandson, Thomas Jefferson Randolph, the bearer of this letter, on a journey to the North, will pass two or three days, perhaps, in Washington. I cannot permit him to do this without presenting him to a friend of so long standing, whom I consider as the strictest of our models of genuine republicanism. Let him be able to say, when you are gone, but not forgotten, that he had seen Nathaniel Macon, upon whose tomb will be written, *Ultimus Romanorum!*" I only ask you to give him a hearty shake of the hand, on my account, as well as his own, assuring you he merits it as a citizen, to which I will add my unceasing affection to yourself." A no less honorable tribute to his worth was paid by that distinguished statesman and honored and favorite son of Georgia, George M. Troup, long his political associate and intimate friend. In 1824, Wm. H. Crawford was the selected candidate for the Presidency, of the State-Rights Republican Party. His friends became alarmed at his rapidly declining health, and feared his disease might prove fatal or otherwise disqualify him. "In this unfortunate event," writes Mr. Troup, to Mr. Macon, in June, 1824, "I know of no person who would unite so extensively the public sentiment of the southern country in his favor as yourself. In such an unhappy result, therefore, unless you forbid it, I will take the liberty to propagate my opinion as diffusively as I can.

"In the administration of the general government we want *Virtue!* Virtue!! VIRTUE!!!"

Of Mr. Macon's claims to distinction, and to take rank on the roll of fame among the first of those who embellish the pages of American history — that sagacious statesman, John Randolph, of Roanoke, whose perception of character was rarely at fault, in a letter to Mr. Macon, 14th December, 1828, thus speaks: "Your kind letter of the 10th is just now received. Many, many thanks for it. I am truly concerned at, the causes which justly occasion you uneasiness; yet, when I reflect, I know of no man in the United States whom I would so soon be as yourself. There is no one who stands so fair in the public estimation; and, with the single exception of General Washington, there is not one of your times who will stand so fair with Posterity as yourself. There are various sorts of reputations in the world. Some are obtained by cringing and puffing, some are actually begged for and given as an alms to importunity, some are carried by sheer impudence. No one has had a better opportunity of observing this than yourself; and there is no keener observer."

Upon such testimonials as these from such high and pure sources, the reputation of this just and virtuous man may safely repose. They bespeak a name and a fame which, dignify humanity, and invest his memory with a usefulness scarcely less to be prized than his services while living.

This sketch would be imperfect, did it not notice the suggestive fact that in his latter years, Mr. Macon had painful misgivings for the future of his country. 'Tis true he did not parade his opinions before the public gaze, preferring rather to encourage — not to alarm the popular mind; but often when his thoughts were turned on what he deemed the political distempers and proclivities of the times, did he say to a friend in his own pregnant language, "I am afraid all my labors have been for nothing;" — obviously referring to his hardships in the tented field, and his arduous and well directed labors in the councils of his country — having devoted to these patriotic offices the greater part of a long life, commencing before manhood and ending with its close. At one period he reposed with entire confidence on the conviction that popular rights and public liberty were effectually secured by the Constitution of the United States; but this hopeful reliance failed him as early as 1824. In a debate, at that period, in the Senate of the United States, on the bill for a subscription to the Delaware and Chesapeake Canal, Mr. Macon said, "He rose with a full heart, to take his last farewell of an old friend that he had always admired and loved; (he meant the Constitution of the United States) ... In times of old, whenever any question touching the Constitution was brought forward, it was discussed day after day; that time was now passed ... Do a little now and a little then, and by-and-by they would render the government as powerful and unlimited as the British Government was. We go on deciding on these things without looking at the Constitution; and I suppose we will, in a few years, do as was done in England. We shall appoint a committee to hunt for precedents. My heart is full when I think of all this; and what is to become of us I cannot say ... His fears might be groundless; they might be nothing but the suggestions of a worn out old man; but they were sincere, and he was alarmed for the safety of this Government."

In vain did he then, as he had often before, raise his warning voice against the dangers of inroads upon the Constitution. And now that the direst calamities are upon us, resulting from its utter overthrow and its base prostitution by wicked men to the worst and most wicked purposes — how loudly do they proclaim the unerring sagacity of his gifted and far-reaching mind.

It was in private life the rare excellencies of this great and good man shone brightest. "To be, and not to seem," was his maxim. Disdaining the pride of power —

despising hypocrisy as the lowest and meanest device — with an honest simplicity and Roman frankness of manners — he gave to intercourse and ease and freedom which made his society sought after by all who knew him. Industry, economy and temperance, distinguished the character of Mr. Macon during every portion of his long life; and he was truly exemplary in the discharge of every social and domestic duty. His integrity of heart — his love of justice and truth — commanded universal confidence, esteem and respect. In his dress, his manners, his habits and mode of life, he indulged no fondness for superfluities, yet never denied himself the use of what was necessary and convenient. The vainness of ostentation and the littleness of pride, were alike disgusting to him. His neighbors, even the humblest, visited him without ceremony; and in all their difficulties applied to him for advice and comfort, which he always afforded in a manner the most acceptable. The society of his neighborhood, embracing a unusually large circle, seemed, as in were, to constitute but one family, of which he was the head and guide, and the rich stores of his mind were common property. Such was the moral influence he exerted that his example and precept were allowed the force of law. His heart was the seat of the benevolent affections; and that he enjoyed while living, the happiness which attends their constant exercise, was sufficiently attested by the many of all ages and both sexes, who attended his interment with tears and deepest sorrow. And that he was not wanting in the offices of humanity, was proven by the heart-rending scene exhibited by the lamentations of his numerous black family, when they were permitted to view, for the last time his mortal remains. They, indeed, had cause to sorrow; never had slaves a kinder master. In every thing connected with their health and comfort, he made most liberal and ample provision — in food, raiment, bedding and dwellings. In sickness, his attention to them were those of a kind and tender friend; nor did he neglect their instruction and discipline.*

He was married the 9th October, 1783, to Hannah Plummer, a lady of a highly respected family of his native county. She died on the 11th January, 1790. He never married again. They had three children, a son and two daughters. The son, Plummer Macon, died in his seventh year. The daughters, while yet very young — being deprived of the tender care and affectionate nurture of a fond mother — were left to depend upon his counsels and guidance to fit them for future usefulness and happiness. He made companions of them; won their affection and confidence; and made *these* the incentives to obedience and usefulness. Well did they repay his anxieties and watchfulness. *They were what he wished them to be* — amiable, intelligent, interesting — in manners easy and unaffected and untinctured, by fondness for the parade of appearances. They were both married to highly respectable gentlemen; the eldest, Betsy K. Macon, to William Martin, of Granville; the youngest, Seigniora Macon, to William Eaton, Sr., of Warren. Their loss was the source of deep and heart-rending affliction. The *fortitude* of the philosopher gave way to the *sensibilities* of nature — for he entertained for them an affection as warm and tender as ever glowed in the bosom of a doting parent.

He died the 29th June, 1837, at Buck Spring, in the county of Warren, in the 79th year of his age. Some three or four days previously, he was partially confined to the house — enjoying, however, with his usual flow of spirits, the society and conversation of his numerous

---

*The writer having prepared and published a brief notice of Mr. Macon shortly after his death — much of which has been copied by other writers — deems no apology necessary for having freely used it in this sketch.

friends, who visited him daily, and watched, with anxious and distressful solicitude, every symptom that threatened to snatch from them their venerated friend and benefactor. In the morning of that day he rose early as usual — dressed himself with habitual neatness — conversed cheerfully with those around him, occasionally walking in the room and lying on the bed. It was about 10 o'clock when he felt the supreme hour had come. In full possession of his mind, he met the summons with a composure and placid resignation which none but the just can feel, and sunk to rest without pain or suffering.

Mr. Macon desired that no monumental stone or storied urn, or even an *inclosure*, should mark the spot where his remains were to lie. He chose it himself on a sterile ridge, and pointed it out to the friend whom he selected as his Executor, saying,"It is so barren no one will ever desire to cultivate it;" and directed a heap of stones, in a lot hard by, picked up from before the plough, to be placed over him, saying, "they were of no value, and nobody would ever want them." Thus, exhibiting towards the closing scenes of life the same unpretending modesty, and scrupulous regard for the rights and convenience of others, which had signalized his whole life. His own native woods, in all their wild rudeness, received into their bosom the friend of the people, the lover of his country, and one whose example will ever remain for virtuous emulation, with nothing to mark his last resting place but a heap of stones which his friends and neighbors, in sad rivalry, piled up over him.

Such was Nathaniel Macon of North Carolina — the kind neighbor — the warm-hearted friend — the affectionate relative — the fearless advocate of public liberty — the enlightened statesman — the just man. He is gone, but his memory lives in the hearts and affections of his countrymen, and in the recorded pages of his country's History.

The writer of this knew him well, and is happy in being able to pay this imperfect tribute of affection and gratitude to the memory of one, who was both his friend and instructor, and feels a pride in acknowledging his lasting indebtedness for the many advantages derived from his lessons of wisdom and experience during a long period of uninterrupted friendship and intimacy.

Poplar Mount,
2nd July, 1862.

NOTE.

There has been no purpose to review the public life of Mr. Macon; that will become the pleasing task of the future Historian. But, it is proper, on this occasion, in justice to him and to historic truth, to correct a mistake (doubtless unintentional,) in regard to his course on what is so well known as the *Missouri Compromise*, committed by Mr. Benton in his "Thirty Years View." In that valuable work, p. 8, the author says, "This Compromise was sustained by the united voices of the Southern Senators," and that "the unanimity of the slave States in the Senate, where the measure originated, is shown by its journal, not on the motion to insert the section constituting the Compromise (for on that motion the yeas and nays were not taken,) but on the motion to strike it out, when they were taken, and showed 30 votes for the Compromise and 15 against it, every one of the latter from non-slaveholding States: the former comprehending every slave State vote present, and a few from the North," He then gives a list of the Senators claimed to be for the *Compromise*, and among them Mr. Macon. It is submitted that this view is not sustained by the Journal of the Senate, as the following examination will show.

In the Session of 1819-'20, as early as 3rd January, 1820, a bill for the admission of the State of *Maine* into the Union passed the House of Representatives; and in the Senate, a committee, to which it was referred, reported as an *amendment*, a clause admitting also *Missouri* on an equal footing. An instant attempt was made to separate the two bills, but failed: (Mr. Macon both spoke and voted in favor of the conjunction,) and various propositions were also made to exclude slavery from *Missouri*, which likewise failed. Whereupon, *Mr. Thomas, of Illinois*, moved to insert a farther amendment, as an 8th Section, excluding slavery from all territory acquired under the name of *Louisiana*, which lies North of 36° 80' North Latitude, not included within the limits of *Missouri*. This is the far-famed *Missouri Compromise*, and here is a motion to *insert* it by a Northern member, and, upon which, the *ayes and noes were called*, and resulted, *ayes 34, noes 10*, (every man voting,) *Mr. Macon* in the negative. See Journal 1819-'20, page 166. The question then recurred, "shall the amendments be engrossed and the bill read a third time as amended?" It was carried in the affirmative — ayes 24, noes 20; *Mr. Macon* again in the negative — only one other Southern member voting with him — Judge Smith, of South Carolina. See Journal, page 166, 1819-'20. Here then, we see Mr. Macon, anxious as he was to admit both States, voting with all Northern members except one, to reject the bill — that is against the admission of both *Maine* and *Missouri*, because the Compromise Section had been agreed to; for the bill, without that Section, would have been precisely what he desired. But this is not all. When the bill was returned to the Senate from the House of Representatives, with their disagreement to the amendments, and a motion was made to *recede*, we find that *Mr. Macon* called for a division, which being agreed to, the question was first taken on receding from so much of the amendments as provides for the admission of *Missouri without restriction* — ayes 21, noes 23. *Mr. Macon* voting *no*; in effect against separating the bills. The question was then taken on receding from the 8th Section, (the Compromise,) *ayes 11, noes 33. Mr. Macon* voting aye — in effect to *strike out* the Compromise Section. (See Journal 1819-'20, page 189,) that is to reject it. A committee of conference was then appointed, and in their report on 2nd March recommended that the Senate recede from their amendments to the *Maine* Bill, and that the two Houses strike out of the *Missouri* Bill the 4th Section, restricting slavery in that State, and insert a new Section prohibiting slavery North of 36° 30' North Latitude — substantially to separate the two bills, and to render the *Missouri* Bill precisely what it was when it passed the Senate as a part of the *Maine* Bill, and against which Mr. Macon voted. At this stage, the Senate proceeded to consider the bill for the admission of *Missouri*, which had passed the House of Representatives with a *slavery restriction*. This restriction being stricken out, *Mr. Thomas, of Illinois*, moved to insert a new Section prohibiting slavery North of 36° 30' North Latitude, (the same, *totidem verbis*, he had offered to the Maine bill, as the 8th Section, which had passed the Senate, and upon which the sense of the Senate had been three several times had. Mr. Macon always in *opposition* to it.) This was agreed to without a division. It was acquiesced in, no doubt, with a tacit understanding that the previous votes of members should be received us indicating their respective opinions, for it is worthy of note, that in the Senate, frivolous calls for the *ayes* and *noes* were never indulged in. Members abstained from vexing the ear and patience of the Body with such calls upon questions which had been solemnly and deliberately decided. It being thus agreed to, (just as Mr. Benton states,) a motion was made to strike it out, (as Mr. Benton also states,) by *Mr. Trimble, of Ohio*, but it was not *simply* a motion to strike out the compromise Section, but to *strike out* so much of the Section as prohibited slavery *only* North of 36° 30' North Latitude, and to insert a clause prohibiting it *South as well as North of the line*. The clause proposed to be stricken out, and that to be *inserted*, equally affirmed the principle of *prohibition*: so that an affirmative or negative vote would alike have sanctioned the power. It was carried in the negative — ayes 12, noes 30. See Journal, page 202. Mr. Macon voted *no*: preferring, if the *power was to be usurped*, that its application should be confined to the narrowest limits; and it would seem that no ingenuity could torture this vote into an approval of "The Compromise." That this is the motion upon which Mr. Benton relies to show "The unanimity of the slave

States" is obvious, *because* the number of negative votes (30) he states, and the list furnished by him of members so voting, exactly correspond with the Journal, (he commits a slight oversight in stating the yeas to be 15, making the number of Senators 45, when there were but 44, all told,) and *because* this was the only motion, at any stage of the bill, or at *any time*, in the progress of the controversy. "To strike out," in any sense, the Compromise Section. If this, then, is the authority relied upon by the author of "30 Years View," (and it seems that there is no other,) there is an insuperable difficulty in concurring in his conclusions.

In addition, it is proper to state, that Mr. Macon participated early in the debate on this exciting subject: and in the course of his remarks said, that "The gentleman from Rhode Island, Mr. Bnrrill, seemed to think the question about slaves ought to be touched very delicately. He did touch it so: *but there is no power in the General Government to touch it in any way.*" It is hardly to be supposed, that, with this conviction, he would impugn the doctrines of his whole life by assenting to the exercise of a power whose existence he denied. He looked within for the rule of right; and, his judgment sanctioning, no extraneous circumstances, however pressing, be they of expediency or of entreaty, could induce him to swerve from it.

The record, then, is the witness to Mr. Macon's position on the "Missouri Compromise;" and it is offered in entire confidence, that it affords indisputable proof that position was one of *determined and persistent opposition*.

E.

~ Illustrations ~

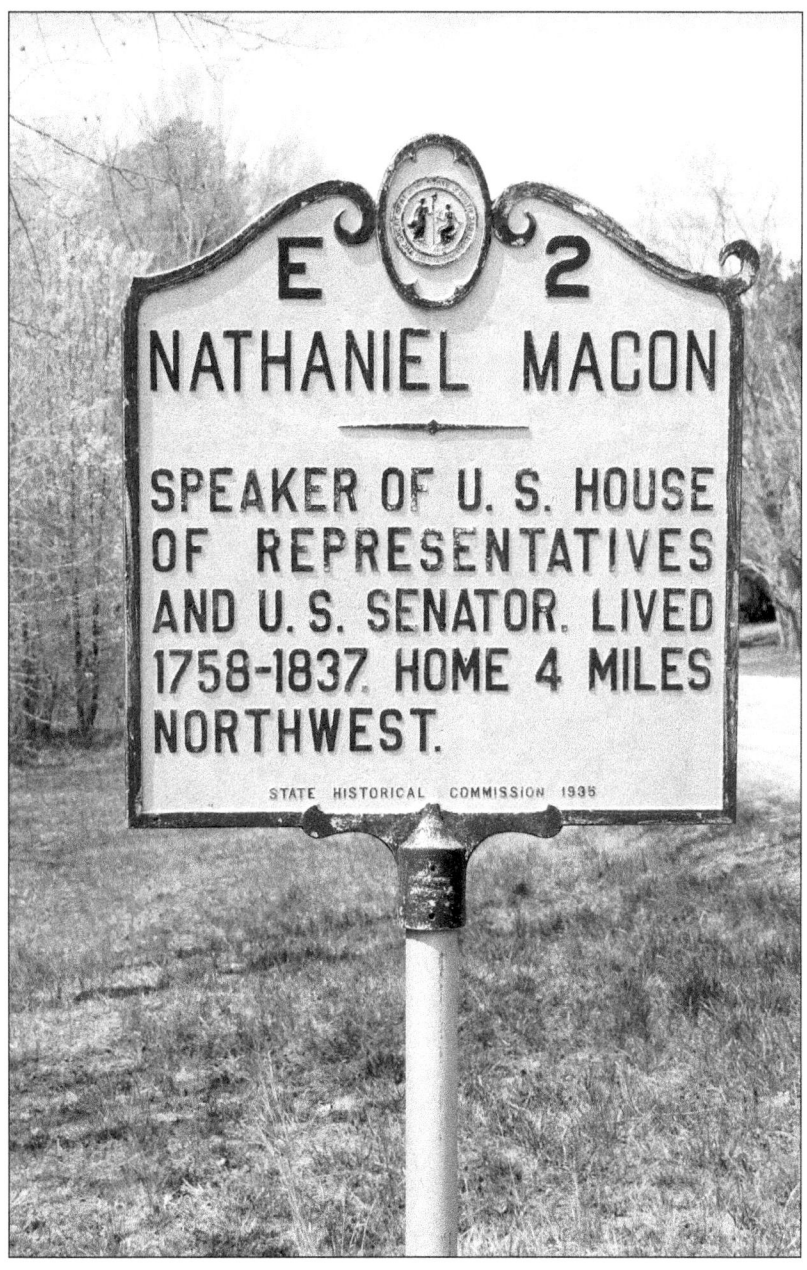

North Carolina historical maker on Highway 158 in Northeastern Warren County, NC.

A close up view of the marker placed at Macon's grave site in 1919 (On opposite page). His wish was only for stones to mark his final resting place.

This pile of stones is the site of Macon's grave. His wife and his son are buried on either side of him and are also covered with stones.

A replica of Macon's home in present day Buck Spring Park, located on the site of Buck Spring Plantation, the home place of Nathaniel Macon.

This memorial to Macon is on the site of the Battle of Guilford Courthouse near Greensboro, NC.

Other publications from

The Scuppernong Press

Lincoln As The South Should Know Him
.... O.W. Blacknall

Truth of the War Conspiracy of 1861
.... H. W. Johnstone

A Story Behind Every Stone
.... Charles E. Purser

As You May Never See Us Again
.... Joel Craig and Sharlene Baker

Another Look at Six Myths in The Lost Cause
.... Richard Lee Montgomery

Southern Fried Ramblings with Grits and All the Fixin's
.... Mark Vogl

Additional Information and Amendments to the North Carolina Troops 1861 – 1865 Volume I .... Charles E. Purser

More information available at
www.scuppernongpress.com

The Scuppernong Press
PO Box 1724
Wake Forest, NC 27588

www.ingramcontent.com/pod-product-compliance
Lightning Source LLC
Chambersburg PA
CBHW051959290426
44110CB00015B/2305